In the end it
Matter
The philosophical
Writings and words
of

Uno Annalon

About the author

Uno Annalon is an Englishman from the city of Portsmouth in the UK. From the age of 14 he was writing and playing his own songs. In his late teens his music became very much the focus of his life and saw him playing in many bands as guitarist and lead singer. He has written and recorded some 9 albums 2 that were considered his best were, Torr stories' 'one more for the heart' that can still be bought online. After playing a 'live' open air concert in 2000 to 15000 people he decided to give up playing 'live' and left the UK to live in Hungary. But later in 2005/8 we saw him playing 4 concerts in the city of Eger in Hungary. Now as an English teacher Uno lives in Poland (at the time of this review) where he still writes and records and also teachers. This book of his writings comes about after many writings on his media page where it was suggested they go into a book. Uno continues to write songs and words. Books to date are....

Life after death
Growing up in Leigh Park
Children's fairy tales for bed time and anytime
Aliens UFOs and other life Forms
A Leigh park story, Saying goodbye to Steve
2076. (the shape of the human race or end)

> There's a time between the dawn and the day,
> when the breath of the dragon weaves a mist
> around the Tor as it remembers
> Arthur and his Knights.
> A time when honour meant more to men than life.
> For it was Merlin who said,
> "It is the fate of men that they forget"
> and as I have stood in the Dragon's Breath
> I have remembered and so Torr Stories
> was born out of love and honour.

Above words are taken from Uno's album 'Torr Stories'

In the end
in the end everything ends the beginnings of love
to the end of your days what did we really learn?
How many times did you promise to try only to walk
away and fail again?
The seasons came and went money earned and money
spent on useless things we didn't need but to make you
feel better in your fight for status among those you saw
as lesser. But in the end you were no better and in fact
were worse because you didn't learn. Oh we cried 'I love
you' but love was just an empty word so over used it
became silly to use and all who lose and believed of
those who use the word to propose and take hearts to
destroy like toys. Oh we the human race in space
disgrace to say I am one. We killed all who stood in our
way blew it up and pushed it away then we started on
nature we changed her way by polluting her waters river
and seas then the soil and plants full of disease not happy

with that we polluted the very air we breathe. What will we leave for our children's children? Did we even think? I fear not as all can see making money was mans top priority. Whoever comes next was not his concern as he won't be here to even learn, your kids will be born with limbs missing or deformed that if they're lucky enough to even get born. The picture I paint with words of dread don't be surprised that there's nothing left, we all saw it coming can't say I'm wrong I wrote a poem and story a song but still no one listened and the world carried on, it's too late now it's all gone wrong. But the rich man's said 'so what I'll be gone' he lived a grand life of wine women and song at the price of our world now it's all gone.

Don't believe everything you think. And the person most likely to crap on you is your best friend. And remember you only lose control when you give it to someone else!

ഇാരു

Wow God exists: so do fairies and goblins and Father Christmas who is also dating a tooth fairy whose far relative is the man in the moon. Pigs can fly dreams come true I know because a unicorn told me

ഇാരു

Uno's sad words of truth: When money stops people from doing the right thing.

ഇാരു

There will come a day when silence drowns the screams. As we stand alone looking at what we did to this beautiful planet we called home. To the devastation we caused to everything that also called earth home.

ജ്ഞ

When did we stop caring? When did 'being human' mean to ignore those in need those weaker than us those hungry, homeless? Why did so many turn away? How Did the greatest gift 'love' lose out to money and selfishness? Who are we what are we now

ജ്ഞ

Never sleep with someone whose bum is bigger than your own.

ജ്ഞ

The only thing that matters is now. Tomorrow will wait.

ജ്ഞ

If you need a reason to be happy here it is, you woke up today!

ജ്ഞ

Religion is a man made control device that works on the principle of fear, promise and brain washing. In the sense that repeat anything long enough and people will start to believe it, keep going and they will follow like sheep. Religion is now huge business with more 'new religions' starting up every day. So what does 'Religion want?' it wants your money (to live well) it Wants to control your mind so that you will always fear 'hell' and keep giving to protect yourselves. All religion is the same call it whatever name you wish but in the end all the same. If you want to believe in something believe in yourself. No one needs a friggin god to be a good person and as for 'heaven and hell' wakeup you fools there is nothing there.

ೞೞ

If you want true lasting love, look with your heart not with your eyes and don't let age be a factor. Love has no age love has no look, it's a feeling a gift. Love and light

ೞೞ

Sometimes we carry so much in our heads that if it was shopping we would need a lorry. People live your truth anyone or thing that brings you down leave well alone move on. Sometimes it's better to lose than to win, to be free you must first free yourself from those who seek only to hurt you and bring you down.

৪৩

Why do we have to grow up and get old? Why is life filled with so much pain? Watching all you knew and loved change watching those you love pass and return to the cosmos. All those beautiful people from the 70s 80s 90s ext those people who shared my life my time who filled me with love and dreams. Girls I kissed and loved all now but a memory. Those who still live but can't be found those who I dearly want to touch again who faces told a truth of what we all were. Isn't it strange how tears of youth are so different from tears of adulthood everything meant so much more back then? Its life some say. But no it was much more it was the reason I am still here those people were, and are still my reason. What I and all those back then lost was 'truth' now we live on memories of the past and at the same time try to live in the here and now with all the crap around us from people who mean nothing to us but who try to mean something. We can never go back and that's the sadness part because that was the best part of it all. Yes! I know life is about stages but it doesn't mean all stages are as good as or better than the last. It is I think a strange and sad education or maybe being so deep I just can't cope or understand 'why' love and light

৪৩

7

Did you stop playing because you grew up, or grew up because you stopped playing? If you let your life be ruled by ageism you will only please those who envy you for being who you are. 'A big kid'

છ૭

Doctors now agree that the only thing worse than getting old is thinking old. So do what you love doing for as long as you love doing it.

છ૭

The marriage guidance asked me, when did the marriage start having problems?
I said just after the 'I wills'

છ૭

Is it so human that we discover so much so late. And mostly too late to change anything. Love and light next time around.

છ૭

Life is a circle no real beginning no real end. The best you can do is "love" the worst is "hate" look at the stars at night like a million poets words waiting for you to read.

෨ඓ

Stress: The minds ability to stop the bodies overwhelming desire to choke the living shit out of some ass hole that really deserves it.

෨ඓ

A fucked up world: Adults telling adults what they can and can't watch. and elected men passing laws to suit a friggin none existent god......and a planet so polluted that one day we will end up digging up the crap that we buried years before as we run out of space. We have berried billions of mobile phones/fridges/TVs and billions of house old thing that broke, plastic killing every living thing and gas's choking us all slowly we don't even notice. And worst of all is its too late now to undo 100s of years of crap.

෨ඓ

I thought I saw you crying as the light moved across your face. Or did you have a memory that filled an empty space. It's still raining. It's funny how we never seem to say what we need to say. It's sadder that we run when we really want to stay. It's still raining.

꧁꧂

Uno's words of reason & why:
There is a time between the dawn and day when the
dragons breathe weaves a mist around each of us,
making its magic for our new day. We may not see it as
such if our day is crap but at some point we will see it
was the best. Don't be angry with anyone love even
those who
Hurt you because it's the dragons breath that made there
day to.

꧁꧂

We were together 5 years the older man and girl. We
painted the sky and clouds and dreams and fields. We
sang songs of love as wild as fire made love so long for
lust and desire. We journeyed near and far with bike and
car tears of laughter like falling stars. But in the end our
time was done love now friendship now she's gone. But
we see each other and still we know. What we had will
never go. We were we are will always be, a love so wild,
so good, so free.

꧁꧂

The word 'sorry' should only be used in extreme cases
and not as a frigging excuse for the crap that so many
dish out because they don't have the balls to be honest.

ဆ∞ဃ

The world we live in is full of crap people they will talk
and promise. Trust me on this people: if you're in a bad
relationship and he/she say they will change. Walk away.
People do not and can't change they are what they are.
Everyone can put on an 'Act' but sooner or later the play
will end and the truth will be seen. Love and light

ဆ∞ဃ

Its true many things are easier said than done. That's
because words are cheap and easy to use. It is only when
they are backed up by 'Actions' that they mean anything.
Whether it's about getting over a relationship or bad
situation. You are your power promise yourself to make
it better then as you move into each day remind yourself
of your promise. Love and light.

ဆ∞ဃ

Everything is out of balance; we have rock stars, film
stars with millions and millions of money. We have
homeless dying on the streets (480 last year in UK) we
have poor people who have to beg. Why don't these
bloody so called stars (who we put where they are) buy a
block of flats to house these sad lonely people? These so
called stars could end 'homelessness almost overnight
and the cost they wouldn't even feel as they make so

much from us anyway. We are growing crops on thousands of farms for fuel, and yet we eat crap processed food that is killing us all. Governments that we voted for ignoring our calls for change. And to think if we all stood together we could change absolutely everything. Time really is running out, the children born now will suffer so badly from illness's we haven't even heard of yet, ask your selves is this what you want to leave be hide?

ஐ

Hating someone is like drinking poison until they die. I don't say forgive anything just move on leave these people in the past where they truly belong.

ஐ

Every day we create questions in our heads and then look for answers that we can't find, sometimes there are no answers, sometimes just a simple action is all you need to do, to bring back balance to your life. Love and light.

ஐ

Uno's words of warning: Beware of the words 'slightly fluffy' it's posh for 'fat'

Uno's wise words: most people are acting out their lives' that's why they fail. The best act you can do is being you. That truly is a hard act to follow. Love and light people

Uno's words of life: A relationship is not about who is boss or who has the most money. It's about love and truth and being equal as a pair. Love is a feeling and emotion not a tool to be used as a weapon.

Uno's words of truth: You only lose control when you give it to someone else.

Uno's words of truth: you have one life live it now. Take chances. Risks. If you're not happy with someone or something move on. Don't waste your life on things and people that are not worth it. Love and light

Vegans: All meat is murder. Plants live as well! So I guess starve yourselves is the answer! We have to accept you, so why can't you accept meat eaters? I don't bang on at you! So don't bang on at me. And just to add, are you going to tell the fox, lion, and the million other meat eating animals to only eat veg?

You don't need a 'god' to be a good person; you only need to treat people the way you want to be treated.

৪৩

A poem of love

First I saw the swan flying around her sky, before she came to rest beside me where upon she told me of my life. You who were born of heart and mind to give a love so new and full of hope. As you feel the pain of others all around you, because you are of heart and mind. So if ever you start to doubt or this dream starts to fade remember where you came from and your love will find you. Now as she leaves me I fill her words rushing through my vines like water over a fall and I know who I am.

৪৩

Lovers lament

Think of me my love as a swan upon your lake as the stone is tossed into the water and the never ending ripples surround me. It's this dream that I have to be yours to open my body to your love to unfold myself before you. And even as the years pass and age begins to show and we begin to slow, I will always love you for who we are and what we meant.

ೞେ

Still

She still walks along the same road the same track made by a thousand horses. The years have passed time flew, and yet still I see her face in the water and mirrors. She will never grow old never fade all I am, was and will be is because and for her, time will not lose us or betray us but simply hold us in its spell of all there is in love and light.

ೞେ

Once

Once I was a boy 15 I think, at school with a thousand others of 15. We loved and danced and dreamed of life and futures what we will be and do. Then the years blinded us many we lost on the way too many to sad. If I close my eyes and think to long tears begin to fall as their names and faces fly into my mind like a film show of what we all lost. Now at 61 so little of what I dreamed ever came true, too much time trying to make my way in a world where too many were fighting for too little. But I have to say I loved many and was loved my many so many now not here too many that my tears run like a

15

river. I just want to say dear friends of yesteryear I loved you then as now. Sweet sorrow let me be free until the end of now.

ഇ‍ാ‍ഗ

Eyes

Everywhere you turn eyes are watching
Neighbours that never cared now feel free to stair
People at work want to know as much
Look what you eat see what you touch
The man on the bus whose eye go up and down
Then his face gives you a frown
It's easy to get paranoid with so many eyes out to destroy
Even the kids on the street look at you like meat
Your family just as bad we don't like how you look
Said your dad as mum gloats with eyes wide open
And a frog in her throat, nowhere is safe from those many eyes
Who is true and who lies? Better stay in bed far away from the eyes.

ഇ‍ാ‍ഗ

And the lord did say
Do unto others, before they do you!

The problem with people is they never say what they want to say. They always say what they think you want to hear.

⅒⅓

The only person you really need to believe is yourself
Trust what you do is the right thing for you
and the best thing.
Because no-one really knows you well enough to give you a true opinion or advice. You are your power. Trust and believe in yourself.

My father once said to me, if you take my advice you will do whatever you feel is best, and don't listen to me.

⅒⅓

The world is full of people who think they have all the answers
Until its them who need help, that's when you see that they really only blaged their way through life

⅒⅓

Do it today, now don't think about why because your only find a reason not to. So the now is now tomorrow is gone. Take the risk or lose the chance.

The problem with 'getting used' to something is that it then becomes boring.

Life is a circle no real beginning no real end. The best you can do is "love" the worst is "hate" look at the stars at night like a million poets words waiting for you to read.

A life time

In my life I've seen so many changes
in my time I've seen so many dreams
Crash to the floor, Crash to the floor
With the fading of the sun
Shadows fall and colours run
I miss my friends I loved now gone
how I wish we were still one
where has all the time gone?
And how will you find me when
the see doesn't reach the shore
and if I look be-hide me
there no-one there at all
And still there's so much more
All I've said has gone before
And all I had to say
Wasn't important anyway
My words just seem to fall away
And still the time goes by
running rings around my mind

and those I love won't stay
as time runs and fades away

୫୦୧

All I said was 'that's a nice moustaches' and she slapped
me round the face...woman!

୫୦୧

Life is made up of moments; some are shorter than
others some last longer than others. But all the same they
are moments and will end and start all the time. So the
next time you feel down remember it's just a moment
and will soon change and a better moment will come.

୫୦୧

Most people are acting out their lives' that's why they
fail. The best act you can do is being you. That truly is a
hard act to follow.

୫୦୧

A relationship is not about who is boss or who has the
most money. It's about love and truth and being equal as
a pair. Love is a feeling and emotion not a tool to be
used as a weapon.

୫୦୧

19

Why is it we meet someone full in love then start trying to change them? And when we fail in this the relationship starts to fail. Remember what it was you fell in love with and not some big idea of what you wanted. Love is a feeling not a look!! Just as age is a number. Love is love no matter how old or what you look like.

৪০৫৪

The legacy of the human race is we spent millions on new ways to kill each other and nothing on helping each other. With all the money we spend on killing we could and would eradicate homelessness and probably fine cures for illnesses, and have a beautiful world. Fuck the men of power.

৪০৫৪

Words of wisdom: Never buy anything from someone who is out of breath!

৪০৫৪

In the end it won't matter because no one will remember, it is the fate of men that we forget. All we have achieved all the miracles and wonders we the human race invented or discovered. None of it will matter. It the future a hundred years from now all that will be said is 'how much will destroyed our beautiful earth. And to be honest no amount of good can equal the damage we have done over so many years.
Uno

৪৩

If you take all the money each country has spent and still spends on weapons you would have enough money to end to end poverty and homelessness. Our hospitals and schools would have all they need to treat and teach every one. We could put more into research and helping those who really need help. Find new drugs and cures make our environment cleaner, safer and better for all. So why the hell don't we?

৪৩
She

She is the mother the life giver and keeper
She is the reason men live.
She is the nurse the cook the cleaner
She is the home maker care taker
Bed maker food maker
She is what we can't live with out
She is the night time kiss the hug of bliss
She will give all and protect with her soul
She is women. Protect yours love her need her
Show her keep her be loyal to her.

৪৩

England

Can there be a more beautiful sound
Than water rushing over a fall
Wind singing through the trees
Birds waking in the morning
Cows mooing in the meadow
Corn blowing in the field
A church bell ringing the hour
A steam train rolling through the countryside
A cockerel waking his hens
Oh how I love the sounds of the country
Cricket on the village green
Tea at 3 a chat to old friends
England you are.

When the first snows of winter start to fall and the long
hot days of summer lost to us all. There's a part of me
that's missing from an end I didn't start. And it looks like
one more for the heart.

War

War, do you really think war is bullets and bombs heroes
and song? War is more much more. We are all fighting
wars, war of fears war of work, war of the unknown war
of drink and drugs. Wars of the heart and mind war of

illness recover or die lover or lost, what is the cost of living really money? No the real cost of living is 'living'

৪৩

What do we really have in common with nature? I was asked. The answer is simple and sad. Nature as with us is trying to survive, but sadly nature is fighting against her biggest enemy 'us'

৪৩

Maybe we should accept that really 'a bird in the hand is better than 2 in the bush' sadly we don't accept it, instead we go after more and care not how we get it.

৪৩

They say everything happens for a reason, I ask what the reason for the reason is. How do you explain? Something that is so bad? It is easy to explain something good we are only to ready to accept it. But when it's so bad it defies an answer or reason do we then just accept it? Or if the 'bad deed' was done to us by another do we still say 'everything happens for a reason? I think it is too easy to opt out and put it all down to 'a reason' maybe it is just that someone is crap to another person

৪৩

Do unto others, before they do you!

৪৩

Man

How far have we really come as a race of people? In all
our efforts to build a better world we forgot to teach
ourselves and each other about 'greed' instead we
created a race that will kill anything in its way. We teach
our kids to take all they can take. We lie to each other to
ourselves and governments lie to the people. Corruption,
power and greed are what rule's the human mind. And
those who want to change it are put down or imprisoned
or killed.

Beginnings and ends

Every dream starts with a dreamer. Every journey starts
with the first step. Every broken heart will mend; every
bad moment is followed by a happy one. You can only
go so far down before you climb back up, every tear as a
smile. If people think your 'one of them' then that makes
them 'one of those' if you ever feel like giving up
remember how far you have come and a little further will
see you happy again. Every start has an end and every
end has a new start. You are never alone love and light
watchers over you, just because you can't see it does not
mean it's not there. Trust me I know what I am saying.

Only when you love yourself can you love others. And only when you understand yourself can you understand others.

৪০৫

Old biker (or not)

My wife said I shouldn't buy it. Your biking days are done. But it is a Harley Davidson standing in the setting sun. I took her off the side stand and let the engine raw. But soon had to turn it off as me shoulder I must have tore. I won't give up my Harley 60 is still young. But it seem strangely heavy and I can't feel me bum. But I start up the motor and up the road I tear it's so loud and I'm so proud and the young girls they do stare. Off at the shop I leap off like a new born chicken, but did it to quick and feel a bit sick and I think I done me leg in. I saw me mate standing at his gate watching as I was revving are you sure I heard him say running away as I crash into his fuckn hedging. At this time of life the wife is right I maybe have to give in. But it's only a poem and you that know him know I'm only kidding.

৪০৫

The biggest piece of fake new in the history of the world

is   **'RELIGION'**

৪০৫

25

The problem with many people is they are not happy just to eat the meat; they also want to watch the animal die. Think about it!

ಬಿಂಜ

Internet blues

Oh how the internet destroyed our lives
Instead of talking we click on sites
We scare ourselves silly typing in our ills
Then rush to a doctor to give us the pills

We went to love sites to find the perfect match
Who told you, you are beautiful and please give me
Your cash. We bought ourselves bargains so cheap you can't believe
Until the postman bought them and you saw you were deceived

We clicked on the latest news to see when war will

come. Then you noticed that little spot growing on your

bum. You clicked the big net doctor you're Symptoms

 You did write oh my god I am ill, will I live the night?
I write my life on face book for all my friends to see but they laugh and fuckn mock me oh their jealousy.

I post so many pictures from holidays for fun I sit and
wait, oh the like clicks have begun. But wait what is this,
a comment someone writes. Did you know your Steve is
having Sue every night? Go to her FB page if you don't
believe your see the pictures she posted for all of us to
see.

So I've had enough of the internet face book and the
scams. I need to see real people and go to pubs see a
band. Return to the good old days when I saw friend in
the flash and not some bloody computer making my life
a mess.

ೲೞ

For lost friends

We grew up in the sight of love
Mums and dads who now watch from above
We were friends and still are, only now it's from afar
The dust of those days long gone settled
most grown up married and fettled.

All we knew saw and done the schools we went to
and that crazy fun. I remember those faces like yesterday
and it breaks my heart you're taken away.
Remember the fireworks in Oak shoot drive
Toffee apple homemade pies.

Those days of wonder of what will be
Always and forever just wasn't to be
So many now gone all maybe free

27

Free from the ills they carried the pain
Not now and never again.

I look at the streets where we all played
the days at school bright eyes now fading away
a girl kissed on the playing field a stolen kiss
again to be. Your first love will she be?

Oh my loves so long gone but in my heart
a moment ago. Your faces as fresh today I promise
will always stay. In my words my songs your hearts live
on.
I won't be sad that you're gone, but glad that we had
each other for a time.

For all those we lost. With love and light

ഇന്ദ

A lover's poem

When at first I saw your face
My heart and love started to race
Ripples on the waters began to sing
Nothing seemed to mater only one thing

As you turned to walk my way
I tried to think of what to say
Heart going mad legs all a wobble
Hard to look cool when you stumble

I opened my mouth to try to speak
Just like my legs my words to weak
You gave me a smile that said it all

28

I have never felt so tall

45 years now have past, who said it wouldn't last
You woke me up again today a kiss good morning
And all to say we love now as we always have
Were some hard times and many so sad.
But together we managed coped and laughed

One day I know one of us will be lost
But with so much love it's worth the cost
So much we've done along the way
Two fine kids what a family dreams away

In my eyes your look the same your beauty never
changed
An angel back then as you are now
Me the man sometimes the clown
Thank you my love for so many years
The laughter, heart break and tears the price we
Pay for all we had. I love you now always have.

ഇരു

Life for the lonely

When you played the wrong card
And made the wrong moves
When someone else won and you always lose
The choices you had but didn't choose

In the blink of an eye the turn of a card
The Crosse you bear all too hard

29

Lovers lost and dreams that died
Alone you stand alone you cry

Chorus

Was it you, was it them was it life
And what next when it cuts like a knife
To whom you gave to who you lost
To carry on at any cost..................to carry on at any cost

The dreams the faded with every day
The so called friends that stayed away
The endless flow of nothingness
Feelings are lost in your emptiness

Chorus

Was it you, was it them was it life
And what next when it cuts like a knife
To whom you gave to who you lost
To carry on at any cost..................to carry on at any cost

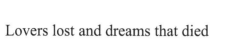

This world

We move through each day
The maze of lies, fake news and decay
Rumours about this and that you believe
So much you feel like a twat

Lied to by your family, boss and wife
Your bank, your friends no wonder we're lost
TV is the legal lie; take some more it'll make you high

Until the end your never see, look as you may it won't
be

Hospitals and doctors alike tired of our moaning
Keep them up at night. They do their best to keep you
alive
But the big medical comps would rather you die
To pump money into their research for drugs already
found

Governments, police the services too, you all think they
work for you
Think again my hapless friend. These ass holes are round
the bend
We are the last thing on their minds. They need to make
money before their time is up. Give to us feel our cup.

The church and a million benders the priests in tights and
suspenders
Raping the children at evensong and the pope bands the
condom
The church no more than a paedophiles dream got the
good book hide be-hide a screen.

This is the world we made built on bullocks money and
lies
The truth unknown to most like the father the son the
Holy Ghost and well fuckn hidden by many. Because
they seek your every penny. And nothing escapes the lie
not even nature, trees and sky our would is fucked as we
all see
There will be no eternity the end is coming wait and see.

31

For friends

Paths that never really met and never knew, like a dream of a wish or a beautiful country view. Something comes along and brings a smile to heal a heart and light the sky. Almost a kiss from out of the blue an unplanned meeting that starts something new. Days are shorter time is fast but a friendship with love will always last. Clocks that tick and strike the hour your words to me were a beautiful flower. I felt each word as they fell and held them all until now. And now look forward to the day we meet and chat and recall so many memories from such a time, where there seemed no reason or even rhyme and yet we were there it was our time.

A poem for a bad man

The only greater power than words is to mean the words we speak. To lie and inflict upon the weak to get your bloody kicks. But I write from the heart I mean what I say and I know many wish I didn't. You can hide be-hide walls and doors and even lies, but one day the skies will open and your words will fall on you like rain. Your look for a friend but none will be found. Clocks and time only go one way what you do and say are here to stay. Speak in haste repent at leisure proving you wrong is my greatest pleasure. Look again my fearful foe you hurt to many and I know you Know with all your hurtful ways and lies well Ray there is no disguise. Admit it now before your own end and maybe just maybe your find a friend.

ℬ◌ℰ

Moments

Life is made up of 'moments' some last longer than others. But whether the moment is happy or sad it won't last long, so if you are having a sad moment take heart that it will change and become a happy moment. Never give up things and problems will and do always change.

ℬ◌ℰ

The balance we lost

We were given a heart to feel, we were given a brain to reason and understand. Our best is to let heart and brain work together to feel and show emotions. But somewhere along the way we lost the power to care to reason to love and understand. We now stand on the edge of nothingness. One day the last tree will fall the last tear will fall the last heart will break. With each breath we take empty and lost, as we remember what is was like to feel compassion, love, and hope. Those things that are free to give and receive trust, help and belonging. Giving without taking feeling without touching. The human race has become more of an inconvenience an embarrassment an idiom for cruelty and shame, murderous, selfish uncaring lost in the nothingness of money, power, greed

33

ଐଓଔ

My body and me

This body and me been friends a long time
Sometimes we creeks and moans and wants to be free
We feel the cold more than before, can't wait to get
home
And be in the warm.
Had a headache the other day took a pill it went away
Once we got a lump and fear set in. rush to my doctor
but he weren't in
Nip down to QA 4 hours later an x-ray
Here is the news I've been fearing the x-ray is fine,
unlike your earring
It's got to come out sceptic it's gone, wasn't gold was
iron. Driving home had to laugh getting older fear in
every fart. Next time they ask for a stool I'll take one
from the kitchen and hit em all. But it's really no joke
being over the ill
I need a quick fix a magic pill. Used to have sex 5 times
a week, every position even on me feet. But now the
years have come to get me, having trouble holding me
wee. To many take outs over the years not seen my bits
and pieces for over 5 years oh I know there still there I
can feel them knocking maybe stand on a mirror it may
be shocking. And how the young think its funny 'you're
getting old'   and your nose is running. Worry not my
dear little girl getting old is part of the deal not exclusive
it wants you as well. So enjoy your youth you silly tart I
hope it hits you just as hard and the kids of tomorrow
will say the same to you. Age is part of the process and

its coming for you, as for me now I just can't be far from a loo.

Ballard of the homeless man

Been living on the streets for nearly 5 years
Seen the pimps the strays and queers
Sleeping in me doorway hiding from the cold
My body is dying, cloths fall of holes

So many walk by and from the corner of their eye
They see with despise as if I were shit. Aar no surprise
A woman came past and looked with a gasp and asked
Are you hungry? I didn't want pity but alone in the city
And a tummy that rumbles like thunder.
She soon went away but told me to stay and returned with
A big Mac cake and coffee,
With a tear in her eye she said bye and left me to eat and kill my hunger

Then late at night the streets and the fights and a fear of getting hurt
The young out of the clubs and all a bit drunk see me as a target
But soon they are kicking and one even pissing on me the poor sod on the street
They don't give a toss I am no loss just a mess who needs a beating.

They walk away but me I must stay it's all I have to live in
I huddle with a cough and try to drop off but my sleeping bags got holes in
So the cold poor's in my body to thin to protect me again
Will this be the night I lose my fight and become another statistics?
Or will someone be kind in heart and mind and save me? The fear is so great
A moment can be too late I am only flash and blood. I just want a home a bed and love.

Been living on the streets for nearly 5 years

ᛒᛁ

And the group of businessmen said unto each other, 'we need something convincing that will put the fear into people and make them give us money without a product' and so religion was born and millions did believe the shit that was abound so the men said 'let's write a book' and call it 'the bible' and more money did pour in. next they agreed a building like no other 'A church' where we can collect the money on a Sunday when the fools don't work. We will lie and make fake promises Molest and rape the children under the protection of a pope. We need a leader who can't be sued? So the last act and 'god' was his name. He didn't exist so couldn't be sued. The perfect illusion the perfect crime. And soon many more religions started popping up all with the same idea...to get rich, kill, control, murder and all in the name of a 'god' who can't be sued. And even today 2020 you fools still think there is a god.

Oh I was young

There was a time when I was young
The clock meant nothing life was fun
Kissing girls and riding choppers
Out to the pub stoned as a cropper

Staying out all night work the next day
Not even tired just wanted to play
The lads came round we hit the road
Got me dope me woman in tow

Age was nothing someone else's problem
Anyone over 30 was long forgotten
I didn't notice the time slipping away
Or me bones feeling the strain

Woke up today a party is on
It's my birthday I'm 61 WTF happened
Can this be? I put on me glasses to help me see
Letter from insurance companies wishing be well
Do I need a policy? In case I full.

It's me legs the doctor said to many years on a bike
Time to slow, spend time with me wife
I stand in me garage looking at me Harley
Time to sell? Not bloody hardly. I will ride
Like the wind (that I have in the mornings)

Now I'm 72 were did the time go

Don't ride anymore friends mostly dead to
Me bike and me did some miles when I think
It brings a smile. Those were the days
Just take a look. But to the young
Don't ignore the bloody clock.

ଚ୍ଚର

We were all born 'individual' but sadly somewhere
along the way some became 'sheep' and followed the
crowd where ever they went and did. This is where the
'word and truth' got lost. People stopped hearing the
truth and just followed like sheep. And you wonder why
the world is in such a friggin mess.

ଚ୍ଚର

My friends remembered

Looking out from my window pane and turning the sky
Into a writing frame. The years I lived and those I met
Now in old age me and the sky lament
Those faces I knew loved and enjoyed, as we were kids
And played with toys.
The future to us was the text day. In all these year
So many taken away.

Hard to put a name to a face
Even harder it is to remember any dates

But those faces I knew as we all grew will stay forever in view
The girls I kissed behind the bike shad, and the days we
Bunked off school. And summer hols down the beach or just
Swimming in a pool.
My first love, oh I see her face her beauty as young as morning mist
The after school disco that slow dance and that amazing first kiss
In love, in like who is to say, but what we had made us happy anyway
From first new love to first broken heart. We were kid's a new start

My friends back then and so many forgotten, lost in time so much time
We joked and laugh and had it all you were my life you gave me all
At 16 the game was over, off to work no more clover or kisses in the dark
And days of wonder in Havant park.
Losing touch and moves away, but still remembered on a sunny day.

I watch the trees blow in the win and remember so many locked within
Your faces like leaves fall from the tree I remember your names do you remember me? We were so young the hands on the clock didn't move
But now they fly like rings around the moon. So many lost but not forgotten

You are all my song, my dream never lost. Time was the problem at our cost.

ଚ୦ଠଃ

Our uninvited guest

She came from China, a little reminder
Of what living so close can do.
She visits us freely the rich and the needy
The poor and the greedy too.

She will have her way as she takes you away
To the place where the dying go. If you're lucky
It's quick until your last click of the heart you knew so
well.
She isn't to choosy fat, skinny or ugly. Black yellow or
white
She may come in the night but whenever she won't leave
alone

Our mistress corona a bit of a loner collecting souls
along her way.
She won't make a mess our uninvited guest. And we
don't know how long she will stay. But after her time
and keep it in mind things will never be the same. She
has friends in high places and plagues diseases all
Waiting to pay us a call.

It's time to act, no time to relax divided we will full. When she's gone we won't carry on as we did before. We must re-evaluate change our living state
And build a smaller world live in small town's valleys and village to stop her uninvited visit. If we are to survive her coming again.

ഇ⊙ﬤ

Life is a balance between you your conscience and nature. Not money, greed and deceitfulness of your fellow man. Did you ever wonder why so many rich people commit suicide or live unhappy lives? Live your life giving love, loving yourself and the world that is a wonder for us all.

ഇ⊙ﬤ

Ode to corona.

Oh its Sunday may as well be Monday cause each day is the same nothing seems to change. But the little virus who is living beside us, you done some good as well, no more teenagers from hell riding the scooters bleeping there hooters and causing a scene. And finally we see the Chinese for what they are trying to own the free world. Well they won't own me. and the rich just like the poor for once obey the law and fear the same as we do. Yes it is a pity that we all must leave the city and go back to life before the war, and all those unemployed must really be annoyed that they didn't want to work and maybe after this will find a job. And the hopeless EU and WHO to whom we also see for what they are corrupted and floored who now maybe will have their end as your

41

money they did spend and the truth they did bend to meet their own ends. This virus has opened our eyes we see through the disguise and we come out stronger too. Boris is the man who will do what what he can unlike Cameron and the rest England will survive, yes many will cry but for their loss and the cost. But in the end my friends when corona ends things will never be the same. But Britain will be great again, so be strong be proud and sing out loud and let the world see. We are British like fish n chips like Churchill and the queen. Love and light you know what I mean.

ଽଠଓଃ
Time

If you look back over all your years. All the music you loved and films seen. Tears and laughter hurt and pain a life you lived where so much changed. The things you loved that made you glad times you saw that were bad. Looking back over so much time, wiser now in different mind. In moments of thought on a lonely day a tear may fall as you say so much time has passed my way, so many lost or gone away those I loved locked in my heart tears mean more now but where to start. Life life life. Is it true we meet again? I heard it said by a friend again I asked but still not sure. Life is still so we live some more

ଽଠଓଃ

Ode to age

There was a time when life was fun
Hands on the clock had just begun
Everything was possible without
Money we had it all. Girls in school
So pretty and game. Youth was for ever
We all thought the same.

A bottle of cider or wine from the coop
Sit in the bus shelter till it was gone
That first dizzy head not feeling so good
Mind was spinning 'mum said it would'

Everything was so easy so fun and care free
Love was just a kiss away a moment to say
Will you be mine? That hug and first kiss
On your beautiful lips I was a king age 9

Then one day I woke up and the clock said 62
I looked in my mirror 'yes its true' age and years have
hunted me down took my looks my hair and even my
crown.
Ills that would come and go in a day, now stay for longer
And have their own way. Never saw a doctor now I can't
keep away

This age thing is a real fucker I wish it would go away.
Still so much I want to do but my body won't
Let me do it. My head is a mess with pain and the stress
And my catheter bag is leaking, my Zimmer won't zim

And my legs are too thin and my ass is like cooked bacon

Just wish I had more time as a younger bloody mind
With the looks of the teen I once was
Hair down to me ass smoking me grass with Genesis
doing me head in, laying on me bed me girlfriend giving
me head. And a life that was really worth live-in. now
too old I feel the cold and I think I am ready to give in.

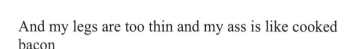

Ode to nothingness

Here we are at the door of 2021
Nothing has changed, only new wars to be won
The words of man and the promise of new
Fell to the floor as they often do.

No new beginnings everything the same
One country wronged another to blame
Children go hungry, the rich hate the poor
Corona the leveller knocking at your door

Friends with empty words still believing their true
No one has time, so much to do. The emptiness of nothing

The reasons and why, All just a shadow bollocks
and lies
We forgot what it was to love all and fly

Ode to nothingness it's what we have made
No one means anything, we just survive
Hardly a life without love and change
But ask anyone why and it's not them to blame

Where once we had friends, we loved and
needed
These days it's net, money and free debt
No more in our lives are people important
Just the need for more riches to show to the
greedy

As you read this ode and say what shit,
remember my dears
You created this. A Christmas carol that
suddenly came true
Look out of your window admire the view until
the poor and lonely
Come looking for you. Happy Christmas you'll
have look back
And lament keys to the darkness life wasted and
spent.

Uno 'words of life: Being In love is the sweetest form of insanity

૪૭୯૪

Ode to West Leigh

When you think of a place that has little grace
But where only the best people live
From the age of 4 never a locked door and never
Were they two faced.

The people I knew and kids who grow
Friends for life for sure. I can still see their faces
Those who past and the places we played each
day a new

The woods and the fields' lakes and hills
Where each week on bikes we rode
Leigh park gardens the friendly old wardens
And Carol serving tea I once got one free.

West Leigh where we grow up the place we still
love
Where everything now has changed.
It was us who were there no trouble or fear
Our world was just 3 schools from one to
another then wake ford

The bugger a school like no other always playing the fool.

So many years past we all smoked grass years have faded away
So many now gone but their faces linger on never ever forgotten
With a tear in me eye as I walk on by and remember those beautiful people
We were not rich and life sometimes a bitch, but life was beautifully simple

ᏸᏅᏟᏣ

To be poor

How sad it is to see the sight of a hungry child standing in the light
Shoes so worn and cloths so torn and wishing they were never born
Shoes with hols coat with no hood jumper so thin it does no good
And yet the rich just pass them by, any normal person would cry

Welcome to the streets of shame were we stand
and begin the name
Of nothing else left to lose no help coming we
can't choose.

Christmas time the lights are on people rushing
to get home
So cold it is in our flat we eat our little dinner in
coat and hat
No tree to speak of no presents at all the candle
that burns is on the wall
No one to the rescue no help is in sight another
days begging to eat tonight
My children ask 'mummy why' there is no help,
no god that's why

We are poor through no fault of our own our
father died now we are alone
We fell through the net of money from the state
born to early or to late so begging as we do
hoping you will help us too, it's easy to look
away and even say get a job you lazy sods, well
everyone has a story some even glory. Don't
judge a book by its cover or one day you may
discover what poor is all about.

The die was cast this is our lot we have nothing
that's all we got
We wake up every day nothing to eat and less to
say
Winter, summer rain or shine. We are begging
just to survive to live a life or stop and die, so
when you pass us by be nice just say 'hi' spar a
little change
Spread some good cheer each good deed you do
will come back at you.

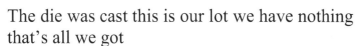

2021

The New Year is upon us, we wait with baited
breath
Corona still our mistress dishing out her death
Poor on every corner the rich just fly away
NHS begs for help but the sick won't stay away

Jobs all lost in 2020 once were wages now banks
empty
Unemployed told get a job but no work is found
all seems lost
So as we step into another year same old illness
same old fear

Nothing really changes nothing ever last won't
be long till we're eating grass

2021 will come and be gone unlike the air we
breathe killing our lungs
The food we eat full and crap polluted water we
drink to wash it back
Into the future we go faster and faster waiting
for a new disaster
So much has changed and most not for the better
I was so pissed off I wrote a letter.

Filling the earth with dead phones and fridges,
TV computers the list is endless
We poison the seas river and streams; the planet
we live on is now so unclean
A million ills await one and all; doctors fill you
with drugs till you're full and if this disease
doesn't kill you the next one will. Oh my poem
should be of love as I watch acid rain full from
above. What hope can I write, I must say the
truth?
Poets write warnings but I don't know the use.
It's all so sad all so in vain the world we created
is completely insane.

I would like to dedicate this book of words to
All my dear friends and some cheaper ones! □

Love and light to all

Uno and Johnny 2017-2021 updated

Beyond the moon

To my friends now gone and the ones that live
on
There is this place where all have gone. It never
rains or even snow's
There is no sun or any moon just a place of love
beyond the moon.
It is the place where we all go some times to
soon sometime over due
A place of love that's waiting for you.

A place in the stars where your life began you
were born
And in life you ran. You fell in love you felt
love's lost
You did everything at life's cost. You lived a life
that to you was fall
Married had children and played the fool. You
got ill and got better
Loved and lost smiled and was happy but always
with love.

Friend's you made and friend now gone, you
were here to carry on
You saw dreams come and go watched dreams
fail like melted snow

Nature on your door step the beauty of morning
the tides that changed
Dark sky a warning. Bought a house then moved
on so much you did been and gone. Life is a
wonder that much we knew but life and death
are the same you know.

You can't have one without the other hot and
cold just like the weather
You are here and then you're gone, there's still
time to carry on
Live your life knowing this, all you lost your
never miss and till the day your end comes then
reunited again in the place beyond the moon
All those you loved and knew are waiting for
you. Take heart my friends
And don't be sad nothing ever ends because
there was no start
We live in a circle where time only changes all
that is now will repeat
In stages relax be happy you are free; life is a
journey for all to see. Love and life to all you
see.

෩෬

Printed in Great Britain
by Amazon